SUPERSTARS OF BASEBALL

CARLOS BELTRÁN

THE RISE TO THE TOP!

The St. Louis Cardinals sign Beltrán for $26 million over two years.

2011

Beltrán hits his one-thousandth RBI.

2009

Wins his first Gold Glove.

2006

Plays in his first All-Star Game.

2004

Named the American League Rookie of the Year.

1999

Moves to the Major Leagues.

1998

The Kansas City Royals sign Beltrán.

1995

Born in Manatí, Puerto Rico.

1977

Mason Crest
370 Reed Road
Broomall, Pennsylvania 19008
www.masoncrest.com

Printed and bound in the United States of America.

First printing
9 8 7 6 5 4 3 2 1

Library of Congress Cataloging-in-Publication Data

Rodríguez Gonzalez, Tania.
 Carlos Beltrán / by Tania Rodriguez.
    p. cm.
 ISBN 978-1-4222-2699-5 (hardcover) -- ISBN 978-1-4222-2670-4 (series hardcover) -- ISBN 978-1-4222-9188-7 (ebook)
 1. Beltrán, Carlos--Juvenile literature. 2. Hispanic American baseball players--Biography--Juvenile literature. 3. Baseball players--United States--Biography--Juvenile literature. I. Title.
 GV865.B347R63 2013
 796.357092--dc23
 [B]
                                                    2012020932

Produced by Harding House Publishing Services, Inc.
www.hardinghousepages.com

Picture Credits:
Mangin, Brad: p. 1, 2, 4, 9, 10, 12, 14, 15, 17, 18, 21, 22, 24, 26, 28

CARLOS BELTRÁN

Chapter 1

LIFE BEFORE STARDOM

Carlos Beltrán is one of today's greatest Puerto Rican baseball stars. He has played for four MLB teams. People call him a five-tool player. He has five skills covered: fielding, throwing, batting, hitting, and stealing bases. Beltrán can do them all, and can do them well.

The Roberto Clemente Stadium in Carolina, Puerto Rico.

Beltrán has had his ups and downs. But he never lets his slumps get to him. Overall, he's an amazing baseball player. His hard work and his raw talent have gotten him far. He's sure to go even farther.

Home Life

Beltrán was born on April 24, 1977. He was born in Manatí, a city on the northern coast of Puerto Rico.

He grew up in a stable, middle class family. His father was Wilfredo, a pharmaceutical salesman. His mother Carmen stayed home and took care of the family. He had a brother and sisters. The family was close. They weren't rich, but they had plenty to get by comfortably.

As a young boy, Beltrán was good at sports. He played all sorts of things.

Los Lobos

Los Lobos de Arecibo are part of the Puerto Rican Professional League. They're pretty good, too. They won the Puerto Rican championship in 1983 and 1996. Back in 1993, they even won the Caribbean World Series. Los Lobos disappeared in 1999. They didn't play for six more years. Then they returned in 2005. The team, fans, and the government worked together to get the stadium ready again. Los Lobos took to the field again to cheers. There is also a women's team called Las Lobas. The team won the Puerto Rican championship in 2009 and 2010.

After awhile, he started concentrating on volleyball and baseball. When he was ten, his Little League team won the Puerto Rican championship. That was his first taste of winning.

He watched all the big names in Puerto Rican baseball. He rooted for Los Lobos de Arecibo. His hero was Bernie Williams, who played for Arecibo. When the Yankees picked up Williams in 1986, Beltrán dreamed that would be him some day.

Moving Up

In high school, he got better and better at baseball. His dad convinced him to stop playing volleyball. Beltrán was good at baseball, and could even have a future as a **professional** player! Maybe he could end up winning the Caribbean World Series, or moving to the United States to play on a professional team. Wilfredo wanted his son to concentrate all his energy on this goal.

At first, Beltrán played shortstop. Then he switched to center field when he had to replace a teammate. There, he found his calling.

All through high school, he worked on improving his hitting, catching, and throwing. It paid off. Pretty soon, **scouts** were taking notice. By 1995, several teams were seriously considering him.

Beltrán graduated from Fernando Callejas High School in 1995. Anything could happen next. He held his breath.

At eighteen, he was picked in the second round of drafts. He was now working for the Kansas City Royals!

The Royals didn't put him in the big leagues right away. They wanted to give him some practice in the minors first. After all, he was only 18. He hadn't ever played professionally before.

Moving Around the Minors

That spring, Beltrán started in the Royal's Gulf Coast League. He did pretty well his first year. He played in 50 games, batting .278 and holding his own in center field. In fact, he was named one of the top ten prospects in the Gulf Coast League. Things were looking up.

Beltrán's first year in the United States was a little rough, though. He didn't speak English yet. He didn't know many people. It was hard to be away from home. But doing well at playing the game certainly helped a lot!

In 1996, he moved around. He started the season with the Lansing Lugnuts, part of the Midwest League. He didn't do so well there. Then he was moved to the Spokane Indians in the Northwest League.

He did better in Spokane. The Royals were confident that he would prove to play well enough for the big leagues. Others took note of Beltrán, too. *Baseball America* rated him as the club's second-best **minor league** player in the country.

In 1997, Beltrán moved yet again. This time, he was playing for Wilmington Blue Rocks. They belong to the Class A Carolina League. This

In 1995, Carlos was named one of the ten best prospects.

In 1998, Beltrán started to play for the Kansas City Royals.

league was more challenging. It meant that the Royals were really looking at Beltrán.

He didn't let his new team down. He was named as the best defensive out-fielder in the Carolina League that year.

Beltrán was getting closer and closer to the **Major Leagues**. In 1998, he started the season in Wilmington again. In June, he was named the league's Player of the Month. He was batting .323 with 20 **RBIs** and 3 homeruns.

His good playing kept him moving. Next, it was on to the Wichita Wranglers, which was even more competitive. Beltrán was batting .352, sunk 14 home runs, and boasted 44 RBIs. Things just got better and better!

Jump

Finally, Beltrán had proved that he had what it takes to play professionally. The Kansas City Royals weren't doing very well during the 1998 season. They need-ed all the help they could get. So they looked to the minor leagues.

Partway through the season, they brought Beltrán to Kansas City. In his

The Minor Leagues

Most baseball players don't go right from school to the Major Leagues. It's usually better when they can get some practice in the minor leagues first. The minor leagues operate in a bunch of countries, including Puerto Rico, the United States, Canada, Mexico, and the Dominican Republic.

Minor league teams form relationships with Major League teams. The Major Leagues look at the minor league players and decide who could play on their team. Sometimes the minor league teams are called "farm" teams. They "grow" players for the team they're affiliated with. Some of the relationships last a long time and some only last a couple years.

very first game, he got a hit. Pretty soon after, he hit two triples in just one game. The Royals were happy with their choice.

Beltrán was just starting his career. He didn't know where it would take him, but he knew it would be exciting.

Chapter 2

BUILDING UP A CAREER

Carlos Beltrán had made his way from Puerto Rico to the American minor leagues. Now he was starting out in the Majors. He was ready to prove that he could be one of the best players on the field.

———————————————————————

Bernie Williams.

The Royals

The Kansas City Royals weren't the best team in the nation. They hadn't been doing very well at all during the 1990s. They hoped that young minor league players like Beltrán could help them start winning some more games.

During his first season, Beltrán played in 14 games. That wasn't many, but he started playing for the Royals partway through the season. He also had to show that he could keep playing well in the Majors. He was feeling a lot of pressure. There were bigger audiences now. The games were on TV. Luckily, he proved that he could handle it.

Beltrán vowed to make 1999 a great season. It was going to be his first full season in the Majors. He worked hard and gained confidence.

Beltrán had taught himself to switch-hit in the minors. That way he could bat either right- or left-handed. He could take on any pitcher. His hero Bernie Williams, who was also a switch-hitter, inspired him. Learning was hard, but it made him a better player in the end.

The effort Beltrán put into improving his hitting was obvious when he was just starting out with the Royals. He had a great *batting average*. He was third in the batting order, which meant that the Royals trusted him to help them score.

During the season, Beltrán batted .298, had 108 RBIs, 22 homeruns, and 27 stolen bases. On top of that, he was a

Bernie Williams

One of Beltrán's heroes is Bernie Williams. The young Williams went to a music high school in Puerto Rico. For a while, he wanted to be a professional musician. But he was also a good baseball player. He eventually chose baseball, at least at first. When he was 17, he signed with the New York Yankees.

Williams played in the minor leagues for a while. He taught himself to switch hit. When he made it to the Major Leagues, it took him some time to find his stride. After a couple years, he started to amaze the crowds. His lifetime stats are impressive and helped lead the Yankees to World Series' wins several times.

When Williams retired, he turned to his other love: music. He's now a classical guitarist with professional albums. He was even nominated for a Latin Grammy in 2009.

Here, Beltrán plays against the Oakland Athletics in 1999.

Carlos with his teammates.

great center fielder. At the end of the season, Beltrán was voted the American League *Rookie* of the Year. Everyone was noticing the new young star.

When Beltrán came back for the 2000 season, he wanted to be even better. Fans hoped for a repeat of all the good things he had done last season.

But 2000 was just not going to be a good one for Beltrán. A lot of players don't do so well during their second year in the Majors. During spring training, Beltrán sprained his wrist. He had to miss a lot of training. Later on, his batting got worse and worse.

Injury after injury kept Beltrán from succeeding. After the wrist, he hurt his knee. He couldn't play from July to September, a huge chunk of the season. He never really recovered. His playing suffered. His batting average dropped to .247 and he rarely hit any home runs.

Beltrán wasn't giving up, though. He knew he could be a great baseball player. He just had to find his stride. Luckily, it wasn't hard.

In 2001, Beltrán recaptured his success. He caught everything that came near him. He launched balls out of the field. The Royals could depend on him again.

Beltrán kept up his playing for the next few years. By 2003, he was batting an impressive .307. He was the best player on his team. However, nothing Beltrán did really helped the Royals win more. He was a star, but the team itself wasn't very good. In 2003, they finished almost last in the league.

The Kansas City Royals couldn't keep him. He was too good. The Royals were a small team. They didn't have big audiences at their games. They weren't winning championships. And they couldn't pay their players as much as other teams could.

Beltrán was good for the Royals. But they could *trade* him for other players that could help them, too. He was like a powerful card they could play. Lots of other teams wanted Beltrán. The Royals could either trade him or wait for him to be *signed* by another team. They chose to trade him.

In June of 2004, the Royals traded Beltrán to the Houston Astros. Beltrán would be moving—but would it affect his playing?

The Astros

Beltrán had played several seasons with the Royals. Now he was moving to the Astros, where he could learn new things. The Astros usually did a little better than the Royals, although they weren't doing so well in 2004.

The Astros had never really done that well. They had never been league champions. They hoped that Beltrán might help change that.

After Beltrán started playing for the Astros, they started doing better. They won more games. Soon, they were the *division* champions. This was the closest the Astros had ever been to playing in the World Series.

Although the Astros ended up losing the *playoffs*, it definitely wasn't because of Beltrán. He hit home runs in five games in a row. During the seven games, he hit eight home runs total. He tied for

The Astros' stadium.

Beltrán played with the Mets for several years.

most home runs during a post-season game.

Beltrán was earning a good reputation. He had carried his team to the post season! During his first season with the Astros, he batted an astonishing .435 and stole 43 bases. Fans were paying attention.

Free Agent

At the end of the 2004 season, Beltrán became a *free agent*. This meant he could go anywhere. He was such a good player that a lot of teams wanted him. Where would he choose?

Beltrán could ask for a lot of money. At first, just about every team wanted him to join. Then, he announced how much money he wanted. He wanted $200 million over ten years. That's a lot of money, even for a baseball player!

He wanted something besides money though. He also wanted job security. Whichever team signed him had to include a no-trade clause. Beltrán didn't like moving around from team to team. He wanted to know where he was going to be playing for a few years. Then he could focus on his playing.

A lot of teams just couldn't afford Beltrán. There were three that were still interested: the Astros, the New York Yankees, and the New York Mets.

It turned out that the Mets wanted him the most. Beltrán signed a seven-year deal. He would earn $119 million. He got a lot of other things too, like hotel suites on road trips.

The Mets wanted Beltrán to do what he did for the Astros. He almost seemed like he could work miracles. Fans were excited. They thought the Mets had made a good decision.

The Mets

Beltrán was starting a new chapter in his career. He would be with the Mets for the next seven years. He wanted to make them good years.

Mets fans hoped he would. Some of them thought the Mets had paid too much for Beltrán, though. Others thought it was just what the Mets needed. Most people were optimistic. Lots of tickets were sold for the 2005 season. New sponsors were signing with the team. The media was going crazy.

Beltrán was under a lot of pressure. He had to do well. Unfortunately, he didn't do as well as people had hoped. It was hard to live up to such high expectations. He didn't do too badly as a player. It's just that he didn't bring the Mets a World Series title.

His very first year with the Mets wasn't great. People complained. Where was the miracle they had been promised? But 2006 was better. He batted. .275, with 116 RBIs and 41 homeruns. It wasn't as good as he had been in the past, but it was good.

During his years with the Mets, Beltrán had his ups and downs. They were mostly ups. In 2006, he made it to the All-Star team and earned a Gold Glove. In 2009, he earned the one thousandth RBI of his career—and 431 of those RBIs had been with the Mets. He was doing really well that season.

On the other hand, Beltrán suffered a lot of injuries with the Mets. His right knee, which always bothered him, became a problem. He missed half the games in 2009 because of it. He didn't play from June until September.

Pretty soon, six and a half years had passed. Would Beltrán stay with the Mets—or would he move somewhere else?

The Giants

The Mets weren't going to the playoffs in 2011. Beltrán was a great player, but he hadn't help bring the Mets to the World Series. So, the Mets decided to trade him. Beltrán agreed.

In 2011, the Mets traded Beltrán to the San Francisco Giants. Beltrán said goodbye to the city and the fans that had followed him for so long. His teammates admired him. He had become a Mets leader almost right away. Other players looked up to him. They were sad to see him go.

The move didn't hurt his playing though. During 2011, Beltrán batted very well in 142 games over the whole season. However, he wasn't going to stay long with the Giants.

The Cardinals

Beltrán was moving on to yet another team. After the 2011 season was over, the St. Louis Cardinals signed on Beltrán.

The Cardinals agreed to give him $26 million over two years. The center ielder was a welcome addition to the team. The Cardinals *general manager* said, "Beltrán is a proven outfielder who obviously has been a tough opponent against the Cardinals for many years. It is going to be nice to have his bat and competitive nature working for us instead of on the other side of the field for the next couple of years."

Impressive Stats

Carlos Beltrán has done a lot during his baseball career. During his professional years, he's put together an impressive array of stats and awards.

In 2011, Beltrán was traded to the San Francisco Giants.

Beltrán played well in 142 games for the Giants in 2011.

His career batting average, as of the time he joined the Cardinals, was .283. He hit 302 home runs. He also connected with 1,146 RBIs. Over his career, he's stolen 293 bases, almost 90 percent of all the times he's tried to steal bases.

But Beltrán isn't just good at **offense**. He's also great at **defense**. He's won three Gold Gloves for his job as a center fielder. That's impressive for any baseball player.

The Gold Glove Award

One of the biggest prizes in baseball is the Rawlings Gold Glove Award. Every year, the best players in the field get the award. Usually, 18 awards are given out in total: one to each position on both the American and National Leagues. Managers and coaches vote, although they can't vote for their own players.

Beltrán has won 3 Gold Gloves so far. That's pretty impressive. However, he has a lot of work to do to catch up to the person with the most awards. That would be pitcher Greg Maddux, who has 18 of them. He won 13 of those in a row, from 1990 to 2002.

Chapter 3

LIFE OUTSIDE OF BASEBALL

B eltrán isn't known for being a talkative person. He doesn't bask in the glow of the media. He usually avoids interviews about his life. He's proud of his skills, but he doesn't boast about them.

Fans don't always know a lot about Beltrán's life outside of baseball. But playing in the Major Leagues isn't the only thing he does. He has a family. He cares about teaching kids.

Family Life

Family is an important part of Beltrán's life. In 1999, he married a woman named Jessica Lugo. They were on their honeymoon when he found out that he was voted the American League Rookie of the Year.

In October 2008, Jessica and Carlos had a baby. They named her Ivana. They had been trying for a few years to have a baby. When they finally did, Beltrán was happy to be a father.

Beltrán also still thinks of his parents. He knew that they had helped him a lot, and he wanted to give something back to them. In 2002, he bought a big house in his hometown of Manatí. He worked on the house, fixing it up himself. He painted, built, and refinished it. His wife and his parents helped him out along the way. He would ask his parents advice about everything. Eventually, the house was ready. Instead of moving in, he gave his parents a set of keys. They had the initials "W" and "C"—Wilfredo and Carmen, his parents' names. The house had been meant for them all along!

Baseball Dreams

When he's not playing baseball or spending time with his family, Beltrán is focusing on his baseball school.

For a long time, he's been working on the Carlos Beltrán Baseball Academy in Florida, Puerto Rico. When he was growing up, he didn't really have anywhere to play baseball. He could have used help training and practicing. Since he has a lot of money and a lot of influence now, he can make that happen for kids in Puerto Rico.

The academy is for older kids who want to become baseball players. They practice and learn new skills. They get to use top-notch equipment, including a field, batting cages, and pitching mounds.

The point of the academy isn't just baseball. It's also a school. There are lots of classrooms, computers, and even housing for students. Beltrán wants to make sure the boys get a good education.

Students get to meet all sorts of stars. Beltrán hopes that other baseball players will be helping out at the

Beltrán is an overall excellent baseball player.

school. He's mentioned players like Carlos Delgado, Pedro Martínez, Roberto Alomar, and Iván Rodríguez. Beltrán also hopes that the academy can host Puerto Rican baseball players during the off-season. They can train to stay in shape.

The Baseball Academy is a personal dream for Beltrán. He's spent a lot of his own money on it. His family and friends help out, too. He hopes that the academy will start turning out the next generation of stars soon.

More Baseball Dreams

Beltrán also does charity work in the United States. In 2006, he got involved with an organization called Harlem RBI. It gives kids a chance to play sports and get an education at the same time. It was actually Beltrán's inspiration for his own academy.

For every RBI that Beltrán hits, he gives $500 to Harlem RBI. Since he hits a lot of them every season, that means the organization gets a lot of money.

In 2009, Beltrán didn't actually get that many RBIs, because he sat out with an injured knee. He didn't want to let his charity down, though—so he ended up giving them $50,000. The Mets matched his donation, so Harlem RBI got $100,000 in total.

Carlos Beltrán is an all-around good player. He can catch. He can hit. He can steal bases. And he has the confidence and skills to keep up his playing. Although he's had his setbacks, he keeps coming back. Beltrán is one of the hottest baseball players today. Fans from Puerto Rico to St. Louis are watching to see how Beltrán will do in the years to come.

Carlos Beltrán is an important baseball player!

Find Out More

Online

Baseball Almanac

www.baseball-almanac.com

Baseball Hall of Fame

baseballhall.org

Baseball Quiz

funschool.kaboose.com/fun-blaster/baseball/quiz/index.html

The History of Baseball

baseball.about.com/od/baseball12/ss/baseballhistory.htm

Science of Baseball

www.exploratorium.edu/baseball

MLB

mlb.mlb.com/es/index.jsp?c_id=mlb

In Books

Dreier, David. *Baseball: How It Works*. North Mankato, Minn.: Capstone, 2011.

Jacobs, Greg. *Everything Kids' Baseball Book*. Avon, Mass.: Adams Media, 2010.

LeBoutillier, Nate. *The Best of Everything Baseball Book*. North Mankato, Minn.: Capstone, 2011.

————. *Ultimate Guide to Pro Baseball Teams*. North Mankato, Minn.: Capstone, 2010.

Sanna, Gabriel. *Baseball and Softball*. Philadelphia, Penn.: Mason Crest, 2010.

Glossary

All-Star Game: The game played in July between the best players from each of the two leagues within the MLB.

batting average: A statistic that measures how good a batter is, which is calculated by dividing the number of hits a player gets by how many times he is at bat.

contract: A written promise between a player and the team. It tells how much he will be paid for how long.

culture: The way of life of a group of people, which includes things like values and beliefs, language, food, and art.

defense: Playing to keep the other team from scoring; includes the outfield and infield positions, pitcher, and catcher.

disabled list: A list of players who are injured and can't play for a certain period of time.

division: A group of teams that plays one another to compete for the championship; in the MLB, divisions are based on geographic regions.

free agent: A player who does not currently have a contract with any team.

general manager: The person in charge of a baseball team, who is responsible for guiding the team to do well.

heritage: Something passed down by previous generations.

Major League Baseball (MLB): The highest level of professional baseball in the United States and Canada.

minor leagues: The level of professional baseball right below the Major Leagues.

Most Valuable Player (MVP): The athlete who is named the best player for a certain period of time.

offense: Playing to score runs at bat.

playoffs: A series of games played after the regular season ends, to determine who will win the championship.

professional: The level of baseball in which players get paid.

rookie: A player in his first-year in the MLB.

runs batted in (RBI): The number of points that a player gets for his team by hitting the ball.

scouts: People who find the best young baseball players to sign to teams.

sign: To agree to a contract between a baseball player and a team.

trade: An agreement with another team that gives a player in return for a player from the other team.

Index